Betty Bib's
FAIRY
CHRISTMAS

Betty Bib's
FAIRY
CHRISTMAS

Join the Magic of the Fairy Festive Season

dbp

DUNCAN BAIRD PUBLISHERS

LONDON

Betty Bib's
FAIRY
CHRISTMAS™

To Nancy and Nell, the original Lavender Fairies, with love.

First published in the United Kingdom and Ireland in 2006 by
Duncan Baird Publishers Ltd
Sixth Floor
Castle House
75–76 Wells Street
London W1T 3QH

Editor: Kelly Thompson
Designer: Rachel Cross
Commissioned photography: Gill Orsman

British Library Cataloguing-in-Publication Data:
A CIP record for this book is available from the British Library

ISBN-10: 1-84483-286-4   ISBN-13: 9-781844-832866

1 3 5 7 9 10 8 6 4 2

Typeset in Perpetua and Monterey
Colour reproduction by Colourscan, Singapore
Printed in China by Imago

Betty Bib ™
www.bettybib.com

All About Betty

Betty Bib collected her first fairy wand at the age of seven, and with it her talent
for spotting fairies and understanding their ways. As an ambassador for
P.U.F.F. (Promoting Understanding of Fairy Folk), she travels
the world giving lectures on fairy appreciation and protection.

Betty lives in a secret location, somewhere in the heart of the English countryside,
with her dog Dorking, her cat Pastry, a whole host of resident fairy friends
and a vast collection of fairy memorabilia. She is already the author
of Betty Bib's Fairy Field Guide (2005).

Both Betty and the Publishers wish to stress that no hairies were farmed
— oops! I mean, no fairies were harmed — during the making of this book.

CONTENTS

TASTY YULETIDE TREATS 12

Have you ever wondered what tickles the fancy of a fairy's tastebuds? Dive in to discover their favourite festive foods.

TIMELESS TREASURES AND GIFTS GALORE 18

What does a fairy want for Christmas? Open this box of delights to find out. And remember, it's the little things that matter.

TWINKLY TINSEL AND GLITTERY GARLANDS 26

How do fairies decorate their home at this special time of year? With a sprinkling of magic dust and a healthy dose of mischief, no doubt.

FAIRY FRIENDS COME TO STAY 36

You'd like to see more fairies, I hear you say? Then come and meet the fairy guests who visit at this time of year.

FABULOUS FAIRY PARTIES 44

Never been to a fairy party? My, you're in for a treat! Enjoy every minute of the festive fun and frolics.

THE NIGHT BEFORE CHRISTMAS 56

It's Christmas Eve and all through the house not a creature is stirring, not even a … fairy! Well, that's a fib actually – they're so excited they can hardly sit still!

THE BIG DAY 64

Hooray, hooray, it's Christmas Day! Time to sit back, relax and let the fairy magic unfold.

Dear Reader,

Season's Greetings! May I begin by saying how **truly delighted** we are that you have accepted our invitation to spend Christmas here with us, at High Chimneys, this fine and fanciful year. You will receive the **warmest of welcomes** at my airy-fairy abode — not only home to myself, my dog Dorking, Pastry the cat, Bill and Coo the pigeons and a host of resident fairies, but also the seat of my one-off collection of **all things fairy.**

High Chimneys is, of course, also the H.Q. of P.U.F.F. (Promoting Understanding of Fairy Folk) — the little organization that grew out of my life-long research into fairies and which aims to bring about an **enduring alliance** between man and fairykind. I am sure you will appreciate that it is a **rare privilege** indeed to observe fairies at such close quarters, so I trust that you will use this opportunity wisely (and wonderfully) to gain an understanding of the fairy philosophy "Because the little things matter" — thereby becoming a **fully-fledged** supporter of P.U.F.F. and all its activities.

One of our grave fairy concerns is the troubling report of **spiralling commercialization** at this, the most magical of seasons. You, the general public, are said to be losing your sense of **impending excitement** in the run-up to Christmas, replacing it with debt and duty. The fairies and I hope to remind you of **simple ways** to bring **jollification** back to the season and to **banish anxiety** from your preparations for evermore. We really are **all-of-a-flutter** at the thought of your visit, as we have **much to do** to prepare for a perfectly **crispy, crunchy Christmas**.

Snuffling Snowflakes! I can feel **Christmas at my heels**, so please step this way. Leave your bag here (the fairies will take care of it) and mind your head — the ceilings are rather low, but we have **high expectations** that your stay will be a memorable one . . .

Your humble hostess,
Betty Bib

7

Our maxim here at High Chimneys is: "Simple pleasures store up treasures"..

... so come in and enjoy the fun!

WELCOME

Well, here you are at High Chimneys, the hush-hush P.U.F.F. headquarters, where many a fairy comes to visit. Please make yourself feel right at home but take care not to step on any unsuspecting fairies.

KEY TO BETTY'S HOUSE

1. Secret fairy places
2. Attic *(a veritable fairy treasure trove)*
3. Yellow room *(where you'll be staying)*
4. Bathroom
5. Landing *(a favourite fairy sulking spot)*
6. Betty's bedroom *(chock-full of chintz)*
7. Betty's en-suite bathroom
8. Living room
9. Dining room
10. Hallway *(please wipe your feet)*
11. Kitchen *(where domestic fairies run riot)*
12. Betty's study *(full of fairy secrets)*

MEET THE RESIDENT FAIRIES

Although we have many fairies staying here at High Chimneys throughout the year (to visit and help me with my P.U.F.F. research, you understand), I also have a trusted group of resident fairies, without whom life here would most definitely be difficult and dreary.

FAIRIES SPICK AND SPAN

May I introduce you to Fairies Spick and Span, sisters with sparkling personalities (they polish them each and every morning, along with the furniture). Neat and tidy by nature, they are most particular about plumping cushions, starching collars (and sometimes even socks), and completing all sewing tasks with the tiniest of fairy stitches. They are, in short, the perfect examples of the general domestic fairy (they will take your hat and coat on your arrival, and you will find them brushed and pressed when you leave). The only thing they can't seem to tame is their own hair — Spick's being blonde and fairy flyaway, and Span's longing to escape from its mousey bunches.

FAIRIES FANCY AND PLAIN

Moving along, here we have our cooks, Fairies Fancy and Plain. Between them, they boast many hours of cooking experience. Fancy trained in Paris, and her puff pastry (something we like to eat a lot of here!) is so light that it would float to the ceiling if we didn't weigh it down with our cutlery. Fairy Plain's dumplings, on the other hand, are famed for their filling qualities. Indeed, her leftovers prove very useful for plugging up any holes that appear in High Chimney's ageing walls from time to time.

As Fancy and Plain don't always see eye to eye (when it comes to all matters culinary, at least), I have deemed it best that they take turns to plan the menus, and, on the whole, this strategy works to perfection. Apart from the occasional bout of indigestion (mostly on dumpling days), we eat in a light, balanced (and harmonious) way.

TY-PING

Next, please meet Ty-Ping, my secretary and personal assistant. I met her while studying Far Eastern fairy habits on my travels in the Orient and, to my delight, found her on my return inside the dragon teapot packed in my trunk! She brings me a fortune cookie with my morning tea, keeps the stationery fairies in order, types 500 words a minute and will be happy to print out any Christmas tips or recipes you might like to take away with you.

FLORIBUNDA AND PETIT POIS

Floribunda is our energetic head gardener. Pottering and pruning from dawn to dusk, she often has to be beckoned at mealtimes (one of Pastry the cat's daily tasks). Despite her hardened hands, Floribunda firmly retains her fairy charm and can often be found sipping cocoa on the roof with the bats and owls when she finally comes to rest.

The little fairy here is Petit Pois, who has come over from France for work experience this year. She's a little green (and overly keen) at present, but after a month with our fairies, I'm sure she'll soon find her true fairy feet.

AUNTIE EVERLASTING

Last but never least is Auntie Everlasting. I inherited her from my mother and she from hers. The oldest fairy I know, she is always consulted on matters of tradition. Auntie lives in the apple tree for most of the year but de-camps to the hat box in the spare bedroom in the chillier months. She will want me to tell you that, in her opinion, too many young fairies live in houses these days, rather than in the wild, and it's making them "far too soft".

Auntie rarely ventures out without her parasol.

11

TASTY YULETIDE TREATS

Here at High Chimneys, we like to begin cooking early enough to feel a golden glow of smugness, yet not so early that we lose the tingle of anticipation that impending Christmas is all about – the perfect way to fill our noses with the first spicy smells of the festive season.

THE CHRISTMAS PUDDING

One of the first things we do is make the Christmas pudding. Most families have a recipe that has been handed down (we use Auntie E's), but if you don't have one of these, simply turn to a trusted cookbook. The fairies strongly urge you to make a wish as you stir together all the magic ingredients and also suggest adding charms wrapped in non-stick paper to the mixture. Whoever finds the gold coin on Christmas Day will have good fortune all year long; she who finds the silver heart is granted good health; and he who finds the bronze boot must wash up the greasiest pans after the Christmas meal (last year it was Dorking, and what a grumble he made of it!).

However, fairies do understand that not all busy households can embrace this ritual and advise that the blue flame bobbing on a store-bought pudding will still attract a crowd of flitting fairies and will not diminish the Christmas magic in any way.

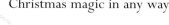

THE CHRISTMAS CAKE

The fairies also love to bake the Christmas cake in advance to give the flavours of currant and spice time to arrange themselves for the big day (quite a yummy thought). If you don't have your own delicious recipe, ask an auntie to lend you one (just as our Auntie does) or look in cookbooks for a fruitcake recipe that makes your tastebuds tingle.

Once the cake itself has been made, tradition has it that Fairy Fancy rolls out the layer of marzipan in which to wrap it, before Spick and Span are sent for to put it in its rightful place. With tape measure and scissors, they cut a perfect pattern and dress the cake with its new yellow attire. This magical transformation is closely followed by yet another when it's time for the whole thing to be coated in bright white icing. Fancy and Plain always clash over whether to opt for a smooth royal icing, with simple, sophisticated, silver decorations, or a rough frosting with plenty of snowmen, sledges and robins piled on top.

FAIRY-SIZED OFFERINGS

This year we put a stop to Fancy and Plain's bickering by making lots of mini cakes with a variety of finishes: a glazed nut topping for Floribunda, a light dusting of icing sugar sprinkled through a doily for Spick and Span, and crystallized fruits for Auntie E's sweet tooth, to name but a few. We have cooked them in small tins (you can use washed food cans) and baked them for a much shorter time than you would a large one (you can smell when they are ready, plus they will be firm to the touch). I can predict that any special friend or greedy fairy would be delighted to receive one of these bite-sized beauties.

FESTIVE FAIRY FOOD

Although fairies greatly enjoy their own traditional and wild food at Christmas, as at any other time of year (from bold berries to magnificent mushrooms), the more domesticated fairies of modern times are increasingly tempted by the rich pickings from our tables – and, as long as they don't overindulge, it is quite safe for them to help themselves.

A VERITABLE FAIRY FEAST

You may like to be informed of the festive food most likely to be pilfered from our tables by the little folk (they take such minute amounts that they like to call it sampling!). They dearly love, for example, freshly cracked nuts, as it is quite a problem for them to get past the shells in the wild (they are also a good source of protein, as fairies are, of course, vegetarian). They adore, too, crumbs of any pungent cheeses and the crispy ends of roasted potatoes.

All fairy aficionados will know that even the trimmest of fairies also have a very sweet tooth. So … remember to look carefully for fairy footprints in the icing sugar packed around Turkish delight, keep a keen eye on your soft-centred chocolates, guard your sugar mice and maple-covered brazils with your life, and never, ever leave a pudding unattended.

Opposite is a fine spread of festive fairy dishes (not including their favourite dessert, which is, of course, tastebud-trembling trifle and has a whole page dedicated to it later on in the proceedings). While fairy food may look extremely tempting to us humans, we should, in fact, take care to avoid it, as seemingly succulent puddings and pies can be stuffed with all sorts of unusual ingredients that neither our tastebuds nor our stomachs suffer gladly.

Petit Pois has proudly poached her very first flower head.

Nut roast

Lavender pudding

Bramble bake

Brussel sprout (or fairy cabbage)

Marigold munch

Cranberry crunch

Rosebud tartlet

Crystallized fruit

Sugar mouse

Daisy dumpling

Here in the kitchen, we see Fancy and Plain decorating a traditional gingerbread house. Fairies think this is one of man's best inventions and some will even make it their holiday home over the Christmas period (very convenient for their late-night sugar cravings!).

TIMELESS TREASURES
AND GIFTS GALORE

Fairies are always thinking of others (when they're not thinking of themselves and how pretty they look, that is!). They truly treasure the act of giving and the joy it brings to others at this special time of year, and know that it really is the little things that matter ...

CREATING A CARD

In these days of mass reproduction, a home-made card can become a timeless treasure. Here, at High Chimneys, we set up a production line each Christmas, for, just like you, we have many cards to send out. Making cards for at least a few loved ones makes them feel truly special.

1. Spick and Span carefully cut and fold the card.

2. Fancy and Plain decorate the front (no icing allowed!).

3. Petit Pois is on glitter duty (rather a spangly job).

4. Floribunda adds a sprig of enchanting evergreen.

5. Ty-Ping writes the neatest of greetings.

6. Pastry and Dorking add their paw-prints.

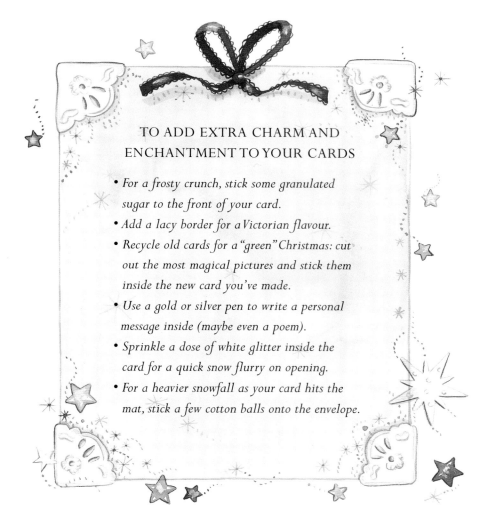

TO ADD EXTRA CHARM AND ENCHANTMENT TO YOUR CARDS

- *For a frosty crunch, stick some granulated sugar to the front of your card.*
- *Add a lacy border for a Victorian flavour.*
- *Recycle old cards for a "green" Christmas: cut out the most magical pictures and stick them inside the new card you've made.*
- *Use a gold or silver pen to write a personal message inside (maybe even a poem).*
- *Sprinkle a dose of white glitter inside the card for a quick snow flurry on opening.*
- *For a heavier snowfall as your card hits the mat, stick a few cotton balls onto the envelope.*

Once we've finished making our assortment of cards, Dorking and I walk to the postbox to send them to our human friends. Those destined for fairy friends, however, have to be picked up by Fairy Post – to be brought beyond the Moon, to the Other Realm. Petit Pois must take them up the East Chimney, where our pigeon Bill (more on him later) will pass them on to the next owl flying to Fairyland.

Magical, mystical owls make the perfect fairy postmen, flying by night to keep all things fairy a secret.

Great excitement has taken hold of us all here at High Chimneys, as it looks like the Fairy Queen's Christmas card has arrived (via one of our much-trusted owl friends, of course). Note that Spick and Span are helpfully hiding the full address to protect our exact location, as we can accommodate only so many visitors. Royal greetings contain more than the usual amount of magic, so I keep all of Her Majesty's correspondence in an old trunk in the attic. Precisely where the golden key to this is kept, I cannot tell … not yet, at least!

And here's the extra-special greeting from the Fairy Queen ...

Dearest Betty,

We send to you our Most Majestic Greetings, at this, the most meltingly magical moment of the year. We wish you winter wonderment and a peaceful P.U.F.F. in the coming year.

With Regal Love From,

H.R.H. the Fairy Queen

P.S. Please extend a royal pat to my faithful friends Pastry and Dorking.

FAIRY GIFTS FOR
FRIENDS AND FAMILY

Having the nimblest of fingers makes a fairy itch to use them, especially in the colder months of the year, when there is less to tend to in nature. Fairies find that making Christmas gifts for their nearest and dearest is the perfect way for them to stay both warm and busy.

PERFECT PRESERVES
Having urged you to make your own pudding and cake, we have no intention of suggesting that you boil up home-made preserves at this busy time, too. If you are an avid cook, all well and good, but I am not ashamed to say that we at High Chimneys have been known to buy well-appointed commercial products as gifts. We do take time, however, to decorate them in a suitably fairyesque manner, with skirted tops of lace, gorgeous gingham or frothy netting. You could even soak off the labels and replace them with your own handmade ones (the fairies promise not to tell!).

PETIT POMANDERS

Fairies Fancy and Plain enjoy the tradition of making sweet-smelling pomanders from citrus fruits and spices. But where humans use oranges and lemons, fairies find kumquats more manageable. If you would like to make your own pomanders, stud your fruit with cloves and leave in a warm place, such as a linen cupboard, to dry out. When they are hard and shrivelled, loop and tie narrow ribbons around them – perfect to decorate your coat hangers and a surefire way to attract fairies to your winter wardrobe.

LAVENDER LACE

Spick and Span have been hard at work, stitching lavender bags from old pieces of lace. To make the sachets more festive they have added cinnamon bark, cardamom pods and cloves to the filling. Place one in your drawer and a sleepy fairy will happily lay her weary head on it (it's the perfect fairy pillow), so give one to each of your fairy-loving friends (or even to any non-believers you know, for they might discover their first fairy in this manner).

Wish Fairies can sniff out a magical Christmas list as soon as it is written.

It is the job of the Wish Fairies to waft their wish dust over gift lists, ensuring that they reach Santa's H.Q. on time and that all our wishes are granted. As you can imagine, they get very tired at this time of year, so can often be spotted resting their weary wands.

CHRISTMAS WISHES

A chunky bone for Dorking
(preferably white chocolate!)

Bee-orchid scent
for Fairy Fancy

Two new wand-warmers for Auntie
— one caterpillar, one rabbit skin

A pink-clover powder
puff for Petit Pois

A fresh, festive fish
for Pastry and . . .

. . . four paws' worth of cashmere bedsocks
— to keep her warm on winter nights

A rosewood-handled potato
masher for Fairy Plain

Red-ant ink and a robin-
feather pen for Ty-Ping

A pair of beetleskin gardening
gloves for Floribunda

A pair of red-poppy silk tights for Spick and a butterfly-
silk apron for Span . . . And, last but not least, whatever
you may wish for, too — may all your wishes come true . . .

TWINKLY TINSEL
AND GLITTERY GARLANDS

Decorating the home with tinsel and trimmings for the festive season is an uplifting and transforming practice which lends a mysterious magic to our everyday surroundings and wins the fairies' wholehearted approval.

TIME FOR TRIMMINGS

The fairies greatly look forward to retrieving the delicious decorations from the attic each Christmas, and this year is no exception. Ty-Ping excitedly tells me that the brimming boxes of baubles and beads have now been brought down, so the serious business of decorating the house will begin as soon as we have given the trimmings some tender loving cleaning.

Crêpe-paper streamers and lanterns open with a dusty rustle as we take them out of their battered Taj Mahal jigsaw box. But by the time Spick and Span have given them a flick of their trusty dusters and mended any tears, the paper fancies are longing to be hung. Next come the tree trimmings: robins and stars, and Santas and snowmen galore emerge from the three old cookie tins: a tartan Scottish shortbread one, a luxury chocolate assortment one and a tea-time selection one. And last but not least, we carefully remove the glass baubles from their three-layered chocolate box. It is always with a shiver that I watch Auntie lift the faded red tassel that opens the lid to reveal the glinting treasures nestled within.

Fairies are particularly fond of a shiny Christmas bauble, for it affords them . . .

BAUBLE MAINTENANCE

Some glittering fairies have flown in to High Chimneys today to check out the lustre of our baubles, their twirlability and the strength of their cord. You, too, should take care to maintain your bauble collection – feel free to stick on some sparkles, bright braid or gemstones to revive a tired and jaded one, or, at the very least, replace the cord from time to time to make sure your baubles don't take a tumble. While there, you could trim any Santas' beards, comb any angel hair, untangle the tinsel and islolate the icicles for a good washing and polishing. I guarantee that fairies will spiral in ecstasy around such well-loved and well-kept decorations.

TEMPORARY TWINKLE

Before we go through to the kitchen to make some tasty treats (with which we shall decorate the tree), I feel I should mention that fairies would much prefer our homes to be decorated in such a delightful and decadent manner throughout the year. They think that streamers and balloons should be a way of everyday life, and I always feel that I am dampening their fairy dust when I remind them that the whoosh of wonderment we feel on first seeing our surroundings all dressed up is a whoosh only because it happens so rarely. It would soon become a whimper if we ate our cornflakes every morning in the company of crêpe paper.

… both a slippery surface on which to play and the chance to admire their own reflections.

GINGER WINGS AND WANDS

Here's a recipe for festive gingerbread treats which create a delicious, spicy aroma as they bake, adding another layer of magic to the mounting excitement in the kitchen. We love the ritual of hanging them on the tree — but taking them off and eating them is even better.

90g (3¼oz; 6 tbsp) butter
1 tbsp golden (corn) syrup
1 tbsp black treacle (molasses)
45g (1½oz; ¼ cup) light brown sugar
1 tbsp orange flower water
   or orange juice

grated rind of half an orange
1 tsp ground ginger
1 tsp ground cinnamon
a pinch of nutmeg
½ tsp bicarbonate of (baking) soda
225g (8oz; 1 ¾ cups) flour

Plus … a star-shaped pastry cutter; paper, pencil, scissors and a sharp knife to make the wing stencil; a drinking straw and ribbon for hanging; lollipop sticks for the wand handles; and a tube of white, ready-made icing, sprinkles and silver balls.

MIXING THE DOUGH

Put the butter, syrup, treacle (molasses), sugar, water and orange rind into a medium-sized saucepan and bring to the boil, stirring. Then add the ginger, cinnamon and nutmeg. Next, take the mixture off the heat, stir in the bicarbonate of soda and gradually beat in the flour, making sure that you mix out all the lumps (fairies get rid of them by jumping on them, but don't try this at home). Wrap the mixture in cling film (plastic wrap) and chill for 30 minutes. Roll out on a lightly floured surface until the dough is approximately four fairy fingers' deep (4mm / ⅛in).

MAKING THE SHAPES

First, divide the dough in half. To make the star ends of the wands, use a large, star-shaped pastry cutter on one half of the dough. Then, to make the wing shapes, create a paper stencil and press it on the remaining dough, cutting around it each time with the point of a sharp knife.

Next, use the end of a drinking straw to make a hole in each shape before placing them all on a greased baking tray and baking at 180°C/350°F/Gas 4 until firm (about 10 minutes). Allow to cool and thread a ribbon through each hole. Use icing to attach a lollipop stick to each star shape to create fully-fledged wands. Then decorate all the cookies with icing, silver balls and sprinkles for that magical fairy touch.

WREATHS

All fairies agree that one of the most deliciously magical ways of decorating the house is to bring some of the world of forest and field inside. Too often in the colder months we turn our backs on Fairy Nature (as I like to call her). But by inviting her in to warm her toes by the fire we are reminded of her green generosity and fondness for variety.

GREENERY GALORE

Evergreen sprays of cypress and cedar, yew and larch, pine and fir are all traditional choices for a fragrant and long-lasting wreath (even the names of these trees cause a fairy's nostrils to quiver).

GOING WILD

The harvesting of the foliage for the front-door wreaths is sure to bring some host fairies inside with it — providing an annual opportunity for wild and domesticated fairies to meet. When the sprigs begin to wilt, the wild ones fly back to their trees, but only once they've fattened up on Christmas fare.

GETTING COMFY

Some fairies find it difficult to rest with ease on the somewhat prickly wild sprigs, objecting to their knobbly cones and sticky resin (you may choose to call these creatures fussy or wimpish, but I think they have a point — ouch!).

HEAVEN SCENT

Domestic fairies love sniffing the array of heady, outdoor scents in the wreaths, as it makes them pleasantly lightheaded (and I happen to know that it's particularly good for clearing up their sniffles and snuffles).

You can add extra aroma to your festive wreaths with drops of your favourite essential oils.

GARLANDS

Fairies tend to be keen "green" folks who encourage us to recycle our rubbish. Spick and Span have asked me to suggest that one way of doing this is to save all your decorative papers to make into Christmas garlands – even brown paper and newspaper can make an elegant and understated version. Simply cut the paper into strips and use glue to stick them together in a linked fashion (after the fairies have skipped with them, of course!).

COLOURFUL CHRISTMAS

At very little cost, such paper garlands will transform any room into a palace fit for a whole array of fun fairy festivities. Brightly coloured ones are the best, as they attract the most energetic fairies, who love nothing better than a good party (well, perhaps a new dress, but that tends to go hand-in-hand with a new party anyway!). And when the fairies begin to tire, they are rather fond of napping inside the paper links (hammock-style). This makes perfect sense, as it means the fairies are never too far from the action, plus it accounts for the all-too-common drooping tendency of most chains and garlands, which seem to hang lower and lower as the party season rolls on.

Among the bushes you may be lucky enough to catch a glimpse of . . .

. . . *Floribunda and Petit Pois in search of fanciful foliage and berries galore.*

THE HOLLY...

"Christmas wouldn't be Christmas without a sprig of jolly holly," or so my little fairy friends say. Long ago a bunch of holly hanging on a front door was thought to ward off evil spirits (which is why we hang wreaths there now), and I must say that, although the Holly Fairies are, on the whole, a happy bunch, they can certainly be prickly if provoked, which makes them quite capable of seeing off any bad spirits that might knock on your door.

...AND THE IVY

As for the elegant Ivy Fairies, we like to weave them into our festive garlands for the blessings of friendship and fidelity they bring (as well as to provide good company for their firm friends, the Holly Fairies, of course). Meandering all over the place, Ivy Fairies tend to get a bit clingy, but their sense of style more than makes up for it: I find their glossy green and cream dresses rather chic in contrast to the muted greys and browns that most other winter fairies wear.

MISTLETOE

We are extremely fortunate that Auntie Everlasting's mother, who was a young fairy in ancient times when mistletoe was first discovered, has passed on her extensive knowledge about the mysterious plant. This means that Auntie has some wonderful tales to tell about it (then again, she tends to have a telling tale for every occasion).

Apparently, it used to be considered a most sacred plant if found growing high among the boughs of an old oak tree (quite a rare sight, as it is much more likely to be found in apple trees). Believing it to bring health and happiness as long as it didn't touch the ground, people would ceremoniously cut down branches with a golden sickle, laying a cloak beneath to catch them.

Fairies like to sew mistletoe berries into their clothes for their magical, pearl-like qualities.

MERRY KISSMAS
Here, at High Chimneys, we like to honour ancient tradition by hanging up pretty mistletoe sprigs in different places each Yuletide. Its presence reminds us of the peace, love and happiness it symbolizes, and also lets us catch visitors (whether human or fairy) off-guard for a sneaky Christmas kiss beneath it (don't forget to pick off a berry for every kiss taken).

FAIRY FRIENDS
COME TO STAY

If you just pop your head out the front door, you will see our loyal pigeons Bill and his wife, Coo, sitting atop our chimneys. It is their job to check visiting fairies in and out of the house. Throughout the year, we have many fairies calling in on us for P.U.F.F. meetings and to help me with my fairy research, but Christmas is the busiest time of all, as visitors from the world over (both fairy and human) like to come and share the magic of the season with us.

BILL AND COO WELCOME THE GUESTS

Bill signs the fairies into the visitors' book on the East Chimney, before asking them to descend to the sitting room fireplace. At the end of their stay, they will depart via the West Chimney (in the kitchen), at the top of which Coo will give them a piece of delicious farewell Christmas cake and wave them goodbye.

Billing and cooing all day long, our much-loved pigeons are very merry at their work, their feet kept at an even temperature on our warm chimney pots.

High Chimneys is a known resting place for a weary-winged fairy to sup and sleep.

CHIMNEY SECRETS

I know that on learning how fairies enter and exit High Chimneys (via chimneys, that is!), some bright spark (excuse the pun) will say, "That is impossible! What if the fire is lit? Wouldn't a fairy perish in such conditions?" It is my job (and pleasure) to inform you, oh sadly sceptical one, that a fairy is much tougher than she looks and thinks nothing of a bit of smoke and fire.

My research leads me to believe that after many years of entering the Earth's atmosphere from the Other Realm, beyond the Moon, fairies have become genetically flame-retardant. After all, their very first trip to Earth – albeit as a mere speck of fairy dust – was on a sunbeam (and imagine how hot that must be!).

In fact, it seems that the fairies rather look forward to the somewhat sooty adventure that my chimneys offer. I've certainly never heard one grumble about the required entry and exit methods, and I'm reliably told by Bill and Coo that many a gleeful giggle escapes the fairies as they enjoy the free fair(y)ground ride. It's really rather fortunate that they are such brave little creatures – I've never met a single one who's afraid of the dark.

As well as their dirty laundry, fairies bring lots of gossamery gossip from the fairy grapevine.

A VERY SPECIAL VISITOR

We feel extremely honoured at this time of year when we receive our most celebrated visitor of all, Santa Claus himself. He always calls in for a reviving glass of fairy punch to help him on his epic Christmas journey, and the fairies flock around him to hear about his thrilling adventures. They make ever such a fuss of him, as he really is the jolliest man you could ever encounter. They swing from his dingly dangly hat, slide down his perfectly polished boots, cosy up to his plush red velvet suit and even burrow in his larger-than-life beard (they tell me that it is softer than you could ever imagine and that it smells of scrumptious cinnamon!). They also take this opportunity to give him some creamy cupcakes to fill his tum, as well as some home-made travel sweets (he is prone to the occasional bout of sleigh-ride sickness, you see).

CHRISTMAS CHARM

Santa Claus and I have many things to discuss regarding the Christmas fairies, who are trained to work alongside him (more on them later). I can therefore vouch that he really does say, "Ho! Ho! Ho!" (in the deepest and warmest of voices). He also has the most perfect manners, for he always clicks his heels together, bows and says, "Thank you, most friendly Betty" before he leaves. Truly, a most charming man, who is welcome here any time.

Dorking has been well trained to wait on our V.I.P. guest and, with a fairy sitting on his tail, there's no fear of wagging and spilling.

Santa gets great joy from the great number of top-quality fairies here at High Chimneys.

Not many establishments fully understand and know how to cater for a Royal Fairy's rich requirements.

THE SNOW QUEEN

The Snow Queen is one of our most illustrious visitors. We never know quite when she is going to call, but when we hear the hushed hiss of her sleigh passing overhead, we know it is going to be a particularly magical Christmas.

She most often drops in when she is simply too tired to make the long journey back to the Other Realm. However, she rarely stays with us longer than one night, as she has so many royal duties to attend to beyond the Moon – from dancing at Crystalline Balls to switching on the Royal Fairy Lights.

Being a queen, she is most particular about her sleeping arrangements; we always reserve her an empty glass snow globe (from among my snowstorm collection), which seems to suit her regal needs. And when the flurry of fairies in her entourage are sure she is sound asleep, they, too, can retire – although to the less glamorous location of the refrigerator.

In the morning, after a simple breakfast of frosted cornflakes and a hot chocolate stirred with an icicle, she leaves via the West Chimney. Coo waves her goodbye in a fluster of feathers, never yet having managed to curtsey successfully on a chimney pot, Spick and Span mop up the royal puddles and we enjoy the snowy scene she has left behind in the garden.

It is not widely known, but a snowman's best friend is a snow fairy. Her pure white presence melts his icy heart.

FABULOUS FAIRY PARTIES

Christmas is the pinnacle of the party season, and all fairies are avid party-goers, flying high on the atmosphere of fun and frolicking — especially if it involves feasting, dancing and the playing of silly games. So, tie your party hat on tightly for a party fully frothed with fairy activity.

REASON FOR CELEBRATION

Christmas gatherings here at High Chimneys tend to be imbued with an extra dose of magic due to friends and family travelling such long distances to come together, often after many months apart. Fairies always bring their best cotton handkerchiefs to these emotionally charged events and can be relied upon to provide a good, loud cry (well, loud for a fairy, at least).

We have to take great care when arranging surprise parties, as some sensitive fairies have been known to faint at the crucial moment. They soon recover from the shock (and the shame), though, especially once all their favourite party activities get under way. For example, fairies will seize just about any opportunity (albeit a fairy-sized one) for dramatic dressing-up.

By the way, please do not presume that fairies are too busy to attend regular birthday parties at this busy time of year, for every day is a cause for celebration to life-loving fairies. And for those of you whose birthday falls on Christmas Day itself, you are considered by the royal fairy folk in the Other Realm to be coated in a special kind of lucky magic. Lucky you!

A TASTE OF THE ORIENT

It's a shame you missed the welcome party we threw last week for Ty-Ping's family, who have flown all the way from China to celebrate Christmas with us this year. After a sumptuous supper of dim sum, some dimming of the lights gave way to the gorgeous glow of our home-made lanterns (see how to make them below). These lit the way for a performance by Ty-Ping's cousins, who (fortunately for us) have trained in a fairy circus. They put on an impressive display of their daring skills – from walking a noodle tightrope to tumbling over the chow mein. So much fun was had, in fact, that Dorking, in his over-excitement, was forced to retire early. Fancy and Plain, meanwhile, learned how to spin plates on top of their chopsticks, and Spick and Span felt calm enough sipping their jasmine tea to leave the clearing up until the morning – simple pleasures really do store up treasures!

MAKING CHINESE LANTERNS

1. Wash and dry some small glass jars and use white glue to stick tissue paper to the outside of them (you can overlap colours for extra festive effect if you like).

3. While the glue is still tacky, wrap some fine, black thread round and round each jar for a textured, wired effect. Then leave to dry.

4. Next, copy Chinese characters onto the tissue, using black ink or paint. You can choose from the symbols above, which mean, from left to right: friendship, peace and eternity (note that peace is so important that it needs two jars to convey its meaning in Chinese).

5. Attach a wire or string handle around the neck of the jar.

6. Pop a night-light or candle inside, light with care, stand back and watch for flitting fairies.

TRIFLING MATTERS

Despite Fancy and Plain's many differences in culinary opinion, one matter on which they wholeheartedly agree is that an enchanted trifle must be home-made and that a Christmas party simply isn't complete without one. Their combined recipe for a sublime spoonful of this traditional High Chimneys treat is as follows:

100g (3½oz) trifle sponges (or thin sponge cake 5–6in square)
raspberry jam, to spread
150g (5½oz; 10–15) coconut cookies

200ml (7fl oz) fresh orange juice
1 banana, thinly sliced
500ml (18fl oz) custard
280ml (10fl oz) double (heavy) cream

Plus tip-top toppings … either a lavish scattering of flaked, toasted almonds or a magical mixture of lovingly placed sweet treats to create a colourful Christmas tree design.

RECIPE FOR SUCCESS

1. Take a large glass bowl and cover the bottom and halfway up the sides with the trifle sponges (cut-up cake), split and smothered with raspberry jam.
2. Crush the coconut cookies into fine crumbs and spoon on top.
3. Drench this with the orange juice and scatter with thin slices of banana.
4. Cover with thick custard (the perfect trifle will strike a delicate balance between wibble and wobble, with no inclination toward a sloppy collapse).
5. Whip the cream into a cumulus cloud formation (over-beaten cream will result in an overcast spoonful), and spread it over the custard.
6. Add one of the tip-top toppings listed above (very fairyesque).
7. Cut into your creation with a large spoon – a successful trifle will emit a large and satisfying BURP, causing onlooking fairies to roll about with laughter. No wonder it is their favourite food!

A fairy can never resist a trifle, so look out for tell-tale footprints in the cream.

Anyway, "Bottoms Up!", or as the fairies would say, "Dip 'n' Sup!"

FESTIVE FAIRY PUNCH

How fortunate that the Spice Fairies have joined us here in the kitchen to help in the making of a delicious punch during this, the main party season of the year. A Christmas party wouldn't be complete, after all, without a warming dose of sugar, spice and all things nice — and who better to create this than these fragrant little fairies (you can always smell when they're on the wing, as they waft an exotic aroma everywhere they flap).

THE CEREMONY

Spice Fairies are an interesting genus to observe, as they very much work as a team when concocting their renowned amber brew — with fun and frivolity as their magic ingredients. Firstly, we see them making a syrup base by boiling sugar and water together, and cooling it slightly (the temperature being tested by the finely-tuned senses of a fairy foot).

Next, they stir in fruit juices and flavourings with a cinnamon stick, intuitively understanding the ratio of spice to sugar until the most comforting (and mouthwatering) concoction is arrived at. Unlike the fairies, you may well have to look up the ingredients and quantities in a cookbook, but, just like them, you will find it hard to resist a little taste along the way.

The last stage in this ritual — which is their favourite bit because it's so pretty — is to add floating garnishes in the form of fruit slices and star anise. These little extras not only add extra flavour but also serve as emergency rafts, which save the life of many a "fallen fairy", overcome by heady vapours. Finally, their task complete, it's time for both us and them to sit back and enjoy the fruits of their labour.

Feel free to bring your cup of warm punch with you as we proceed to the sitting room for some fairy fun and games . . .

FUN FAIRY GAMES

Fairies are the most enthusiastic fans of party games I have ever encountered. They love to invent their own unique games, as well as playing old favourites like charades, and they are very keen for you to join in with the home-made magic and mischief during your stay here.

SPOT THE FAIRIES

Turn back to pages 42–3 to play a game called "Spot the Fairies". Once there, all you have to do is use your fairy radar to count the number of magical little creatures you can see in the dreamy (but chilly) snow scene. Try not to miss any, as you don't want them to feel left out!

HUNT THE KEY

The fairies have also persuaded me to let you play "Hunt the Key". This involves searching for the key to the golden trunk in the attic, where all our top-secret royal correspondence is stored. A clue to its cosy location: musical visitors are singing "in key" on the page where it's hidden.

MADJECTIVES

The fairies opposite are playing a game called "Madjectives" by acting out describing words in a madly magical manner. All you have to do to win is match the adjectives below to the relevant fairy. You could try this game at home by acting out adjectives to your friends.

You will be given the answers to these games on your departure (page 72), but please do keep this information to yourself, as it is important to respect the great secrecy around All Things Fairy.

We are very fortunate to have the Sugar Plum fairy staying with us at the
moment. Every Christmas, she elegantly adds to the party atmosphere by dancing in
the antique fairy theatre that I have in my collection of All Things Fairy.

Fairies always flock to the ballet — not only to perfect their pirouettes and copy the style of the latest tutus, but also to mingle with the magical music and soak up the enchanting atmosphere of the theatre in general (front-row seats are in high demand!).

CHRISTMAS CAROLS

What better way to calm the jingle-jangle of our party excitement than to welcome the sound of traditional Christmas carolers at the door, as night draws near. These generous souls bring musical merriment to High Chimneys (and all of us who dwell in her). The resident fairies waste not a jot of time in getting the best seats in the house, by the cosy curtains, where they lap up the festive show.

WILD FAIRY FROLICS

Just as I thought, there is a host of hovering wild fairies around our visitors' glowing lanterns (easily missed amid the whirling snowflakes). If I'm not mistaken, the occasional rogue one will be blowing dripping wax onto the carolers' woolly gloves and jumping, daringly, through the candle flames. Too much fairy activity, however, can cause the flames to be extinguished, so particularly naughty fairies often disguise themselves as moths to avoid discovery during this mischievous practice. Most "good" fairies, on the other hand, are simply happy to drift amid the silent snow and the magical music, snuggling in the singers' scarves and hats from time to time, with wands a-glow and their fairy ears a-tingling.

Hark! I think I hear carol singers outside. Draw back the curtains, Spick and Span, and let's see . . . .

THE NIGHT BEFORE CHRISTMAS

The day we've all come together for is fast approaching (can you feel the tingle of anticipation in the air?). Yet, there is still much to be done, so there's no time to rest. The tree needs dressing, the gifts checking and wrapping, the stockings hanging up ... will it all be ready by midnight? Fingers and wings crossed it will be ...

DECORATING THE TREE

As Spick puts another coal on the fire, it is time to dress the tree in all its finery. Personally, we feel that there is a certain excitement about putting it up at what a lot of people would consider this late stage. We find the magic somewhat diluted if we live with the tree for a whole month, preferring instead to absorb its enchantment over the official twelve days only.

Floribunda has cut us a fine specimen this year and lovingly sprayed it with a special fairy dust to ensure it doesn't drop its needles (if only we could put this potion into commercial production, I believe we could raise some serious money for P.U.F.F.'s cause!).

Here at High Chimneys, we crown the tree with (of course!) a fairy, and I see that our much-loved Tree-Top Fairy is busy having her hair and dress adjusted (she comes out only once a year and wants to look her best). Unlike other fairies, who enjoy updating their appearance, this one prides herself on wearing her original gown every single year. She is most proud of her faded spangled glory and does a fine job of reigning over her kingdom of dazzling decorations (vain little fairies included — see how they secretly admire themselves in the bright baubles' shiny surfaces?).

Fairies utterly adore the allure of a twinkly tree.

I think this is the perfect moment for us to sit back with a glass of fairy punch and admire the whole effect.

Now that twilight has fallen, the Christmas Fairies have arrived to help us wrap the presents. These charming little creatures remind us why the act of exchanging gifts is such a magical one, as everything they touch is filled with an energy of enchantment. Each year, I bring out my childhood toys for them to assess just how much magic is still stored within them. As you can see, the fairy dust is released as soon as they open them up, proving that the magic of a well-loved gift not only lives on but multiplies, making Christmas all the more special.

THE CHRISTMAS FAIRIES

I can exclusively reveal to you that the Christmas Fairies — a particularly flurried festive bunch who visit us but once a year — are part of an elite squad that work alongside Santa Claus every Yuletide. Without the organizational skills of these busy little beings, Christmas might well have become rather a disappointing occasion or even gone out of fashion altogether.

Elves, of course, are known to work all year in Santa's workshops and load his sleigh on the big night, but it is the fairies who file all his correspondence, map and navigate his route, measure chimney pot access and tie up his boot laces (truth be known, Santa has very little sense of direction and can be a tad forgetful!). Let us wish them safe sleighing this Christmas Eve …

These festive fairies work at such a frenzied pace that they will soon have to hibernate until November, when their work will begin again.

TIME FOR BED

A Clock Fairy tells me that time is flying, so it's time for us to hang up our stockings before heading to bed. Can you tell whose stocking is whose? I hope so, as I stitched them myself so that everyone could recognize their own (no squabbling allowed on Christmas morning). Until then, I trust you will find the Yellow Room comfortable. We'll see you in the morning …

Sweet dreams, Pastry and Dorking … and no peeking in your stockings until you hear the flutter of fairy wings tomorrow morning!

Do you hear Auntie calling her usual night-time farewell? "I wish you nighty nighty! May all your dreams be flighty."

Spick and Span turn back the duster in the broom cupboard to get some well-deserved rest.

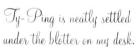

Ty-Ping is neatly settled under the blotter on my desk.

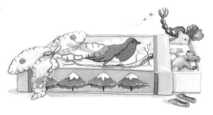

Petit Pois (and Pierre the bear) are tightly tucked into a festively decorated matchbox.

Fancy and Plain are already snoring in their Christmas tea caddy.

Floribunda, who usually sleeps in a flowerbed, snuggles into the cosy coal by the fire tonight.

Auntie Everlasting is retiring to her hat box, well and truly ready for the Land of Nod.

The Big Day

Christmas Day has finally arrived and we just can't wait for all the thrills and frills ahead. I see the fairies have made a start by opening some of their presents. They're up rather early, and with all the rustling of ribbons and paper, I don't think it will be long before Pastry and Dorking join them.

IT'S A CRACKER

Now, with the scent of the feast to come warming our nostrils and teasing our tastebuds, we have just one more task to complete before admiring our reflections in the cutlery and tucking into the long-awaited festive spread: the Christmas crackers must be pulled.

TESTING TIME

The crackers must not only be pulled, but also carefully assessed, for the Cracker Factory depends on our annual report on the worthiness of its products. We receive many boxes of complimentary crackers to this end, and this year the fairies are testing the Sooper-Dooper De-Luxe Range. This is, of course, an enjoyable job but it is also a serious one, as next year's crackers will be designed on the basis of our findings.

Ty-Ping has the task of recording the results, marking each cracker with either P for "poor", NB for "not bad", FFF for "fine fairy fun" or CGC for "cracking good cracker", according to its performance in a range of all-important assessment categories (see list right).

I see that Dorking has come off worse again this year in the annual cracker squabble with Pastry.

CRACKER CATEGORIES

• *Strength of Cracker: how many fairies does it take to pull it apart?*
(measured in fairy power)
• *Loudness of Bang: does it make the fairies jump out of their silk*
stockings? If so, how high?
• *Quality of Humour: does the joke enclosed result in a snort, a snigger,*
a belly laugh or, best of all, a fairy rolling about on the floor?
• *Design of Hat: chic, everyday or wouldn't be seen dead in it?*
(Sadly, crackers rarely score well in this category, as fairies think
that paper hats could be so much more fun.)
• *Desirability of Trinket: performance tends to be significantly better*
in this category, as fairies adore almost all small-scale objects, even
if only made of plastic and of limited use.

Goodness, is it that time already? Fairy Plain
is sounding the gong, so let us make our way (in
an orderly fashion, if you please, fairies) to
the dining room for Christmas dinner . . .

CHRISTMAS DINNER

Invited to join us for Christmas dinner every year are the dedicated members of the P.U.F.F. committee. They greatly look forward to this annual event (safe in the knowledge that none of Plain's dumplings are likely to be on the menu!). Can you hear the faint rumbling of fairy stomachs?

FINE DINING

Once all of us humans have taken our place, the fairies take their seats centre-stage, as is customary: in the middle of the table, around a perfectly arranged platter of their own fairy food. The pitter-patter of last-minute garnishes being brought to the table by Fancy and Plain is interrupted by Ty-Ping, who expertly gains silence for me to make my annual speech by tapping my glass with a teaspoon. This is my opportunity to formally thank fairies and committee members alike for their hard work throughout the year; to congratulate Bill and Coo for their friendly and feathery labour at chimney-pot level (a courteous "coo" can usually be heard from the fireplace at this point); and, lastly, to thank Pastry and Dorking for their loyalty and devotion to the fairies and myself at all times. The fairies then raise their goblets and drink a toast to the much-loved Fairy Queen (long may she twinkle over us). Only then can the fairy feasting commence ...

Spick and Span like to make sure that every napkin is neat and that every knife is fairy-fingerprint free.

AND RELAX ...

Oh, the folly of overfilling one's greedy stomach, yet what relief to collapse into a comfy chair and flop into Christmas afternoon. After listening to the Fairy Queen's speech (she comes through our T.V. set on special airwaves), we like to loosen our belts, shake out our wings and muster up just enough energy to try out our presents or reach for a chocolate.

Spick and Span have used their super-power fairy dust to clean up the pots and pans in one big Whoosh! of their wands, so that dear old Dorking, who found the boot in his pudding again this year, doesn't have to do it. He's making the most of this by playing tumbling blocks with Ty-Ping — he is rather good at the game ... until his excitable tail lets him down!

Pastry prefers to purr from her favourite cushion, showing off her new diamanté collar (an unexpected gift from the Fairy Queen) in Petit Pois' new snail-shell mirror (a present from her family in France). What with this, her clover puff and her oyster-shell powder, Petit Pois now has everything a pretty young fairy needs.

I see that Spick and Span, who, as usual, can't sit still, are busy polishing the Scrabble tiles. Once they have arranged them in alphabetical order, we might be able to persuade them to play a game with us. Be warned, however, that last year they could think only of words such as tidy, shiny, neat and folded, so flew off to clean the Monopoly houses instead.

In a happy, after-dinner glow, Fancy and Plain are reading their new recipe books, "Tasty Tidbits for Fancy Fairies" and "100 Ways with Suet and Semolina", respectively. It won't be long, however, before saucepan lids start to clatter and they work up a steam, trying to agree on the best method to deal with the Christmas leftovers.

Having supped herself to sleep, Auntie Everlasting is now snoring away Christmas afternoon in a bowl of bonbons. Although spritely for her age, she does need more than the average quota of fairy naps. We often have to keep an eye open for her, as she has been known to nod off in the most inconvenient of places, including on the bath sponge (where she gets rather damp) and in the herb bed (where she gets rather minty!).

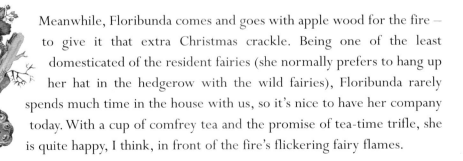

Meanwhile, Floribunda comes and goes with apple wood for the fire — to give it that extra Christmas crackle. Being one of the least domesticated of the resident fairies (she normally prefers to hang up her hat in the hedgerow with the wild fairies), Floribunda rarely spends much time in the house with us, so it's nice to have her company today. With a cup of comfrey tea and the promise of tea-time trifle, she is quite happy, I think, in front of the fire's flickering fairy flames.

Snuffling Snowflakes, what a Merry Berry Christmas we're all having!

It's been a pleasure having you as our guest. May your tinsel always twinkle and your baubles never dim!

FOND FAREWELLS

We can't thank you enough for choosing to spend this Christmas with us here at High Chimneys. We've had a magical time letting you into our fairy secrets and dearly hope that you will visit us again soon for more fairy frolicking, tips and tales. In the meantime, myself, the fairies and, of course, the Fairy Queen wish you a fun and fanciful year ahead (full of fantastical fairy-spotting). Until next time …

Betty's Thorough Thanks

Thank you so much to all the fairy fans and supporters at Duncan Baird. Also to Bertie Bumble for his patient help with modern technology, to my chums Penny and Victor for providing props for fairy research, and to Glenys for feeding Pastry when I'm away on my travels.

FAIRY GAMES ANSWERS
Crumbs! We nearly let you leave without filling you in on the answers to the games we played on page 50:

Madjectives: *The fairies are such good actresses that we don't think you need answers to this game. I trust we're right!*

Spot the Fairies: *I would guess that you found 19 fairies. Some canny fairy spotters will have included the Snow Fairy herself to make 20, but who among you will also have found the secret twig fairy, directly to the left of the Snow Fairy? Look through a magnifying glass to find her if needs be.*

Hunt the Key: *The key to the golden trunk in the attic is cunningly hidden in the curtain on pages 54–5 (so cunningly, in fact, that you may have to use your magnifying glass to see it!). A sprinkling of fairy dust allows it to merge magically with the fancy floral print for safekeeping.*